The Pocket Book of
WELLBEING

8Wise products:

8 Wise Ways to a Healthier Happier Mind, by Kim Rutherford

8Wise™ 12- Week Journal

8Wise™ 12- Month Wellness Planner

8Wise™ Masterclass Workshop

8Wise™ Discovery Workshop

8Wise™ Ways Training course

8Wise™ Pro Training course

To learn more about 8Wise™, please visit **www.8wise.co.uk**

The Pocket Book of
WELLBEING

*8 Wise Ways
to live a healthier happier life*

Kim Rutherford

Psychotherapist and Founder of 8Wise™

LONDON

The Pocketbook of Wellbeing: 8 Wise Ways to live a healthier happier life

The information given in this book should not be treated as a substitute for professional medical advice. Always consult a medical practitioner. Although the author and publisher have made every effort to ensure that the information in this book was correct at press time, the author and publisher do not assume and hereby disclaim any liability to any party for any loss, damage, or disruption caused by errors or omissions, whether such errors or omissions result from negligence, accident, or any other cause.

Copyright © Kim Rutherford and © Dalton Wise Consultancy Ltd, 2021

All rights reserved. No part of this book may be reproduced in any form, including photocopying and recording, without permission in writing from the publisher, except by a reviewer who may quote brief pages in review.

The book information is catalogued as follows;
Author Name(s): Kim Rutherford
Title: The Pocketbook of Wellbeing: 8 Wise Ways to live a healthier happier life
Description; First Edition

1st Edition, 2021

Illustrations copyright ©Kim Rutherford and
@Dalton Wise Consultancy Ltd 2021

Book Design by Leah Kent

ISBN 978-1-914447-40-2 (paperback)

Prepared by That Guy's House
www.ThatGuysHouse.com

The Pocket Book of Wellbeing

Look after your mental health and wellbeing through 8 simple steps.

This pocket book provides 8 simple steps from 8Wise® that can be used to boost your mental health and wellbeing for healthier happier life.

It can be used alongside *'8Wise Ways to a healthier and Happier Life',* by Kim Rutherford, 2021, publisher: That Guy's House as well as the 8Wise 12 week Journal or 12 month 8Wise Planner.

This little pocketbook can help you manage the chaos, challenges and traumas of life through accessing all areas of your wellness spectrum effectively and positively.

What is 8Wise™

8Wise™ looks at your mental health and wellbeing through four core dimensions:

1. **Foundation Dimension** for strong health and wellbeing through Physical wellness and Emotional wellness.

2. **Internal Dimension** for achieving self-acceptance through Spiritual and Intellectual wellness.

3. **External Dimension** for interacting with the world positively and effectively through Environmental wellness is Social wellness .

4. **Lifestyle Dimension** for creating the fulfilling life you want for yourself supported by Occupational wellness and Financial wellness.

8Wise™ can help you to assess your current wellness levels, set realistic goals for a healthier happier mind.

8Wise™ helps you to develop the tools to manage your stress and life challenges to protect your longer term mental and physical health for a happier, healthier and fulfilling life.

How to use 8Wise™

To start living the 8Wise Way for better mental health and wellbeing first you need to assess yourself against all 4 dimensions of the 8Wise model to identify your lowest and highest wellness areas. You can do this using the free tools on the 8Wise™ website: **www.8wise.co.uk**

The tools lead you to create your own 8Wise™ Map which looks a little like this.

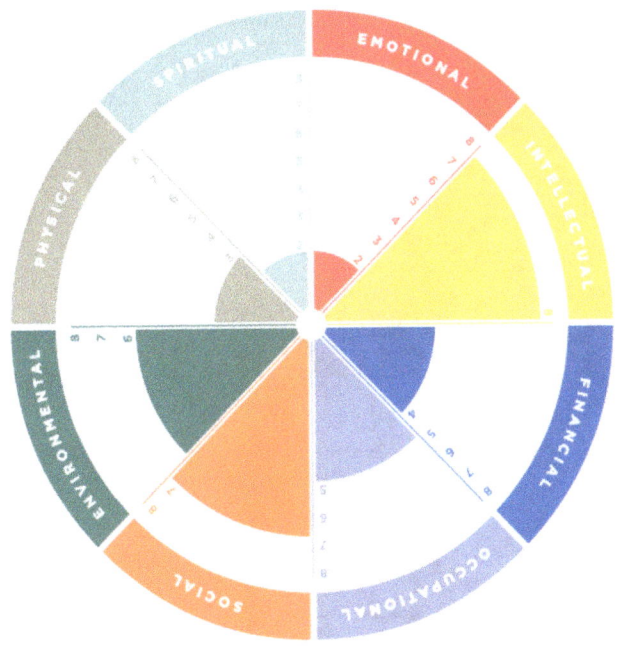

From this you can start to create your own 8Wise™ Transition Plan, implementing some of the activities in this book and others you will identify for yourself to help you improve each of the eight wellness elements for better mental health and wellbeing as well as a healthier happier mind.

Emotional Wellness

Emotional Wellness
Have a positive attitude, high self-esteem, a strong sense of self, and the ability to recognise and share a wide range of feelings with others in a constructive way

Emotional Wellness Tips

---

1 Awarness of thoughts and feelings
Take time to become aware of certain thoughts or triggers that cause these negative emotions.

2 Staying positive
Noticing how often you think or say negative things is the first step towards having a positive attitude - then work on limiting it.

3 Ask for help
Seeking support doesn't mean you are weak, it means you are strong enough to take care of your mental health.

4 Keep Boundaries
Establishing boundaries with people in your life will keep you from feeling overwhelmed by other people's expectations and behaviours.

5 Self Compassion

Practice self-compassion to develop better emotional stability.

6 Self Acceptance

Becoming aware and then learning how to manage negative thoughts and self-talk is key to learning how to accept yourself.

7 Control

Learn to identify and focus on what is in your control and not what is out of your control.

8 Invest in therapy

Going to the gym helps to keep your body healthy and going to see a therapist helps keep your mind healthy. Don't see therapy as something to use when there is a problem, see it as something to acess to prevent problems too.

Emotional Wellness

The ability to successfully handle life's stresses and adapt to change and difficult situations requires you to accept your emotions and work through them in a positive and healthy way.

Emotional Wellness

Emotions are energy that need to be burnt off. Suppressing them expands their pressure and power, increasing the risk of them exploding uncontrollably. Emotional wellness prevents that explosion.

Notes

Notes

Notes

Notes

Physical Wellness

Physical Wellness
Take care of your body for optimal health and functioning

Physical Wellness Tips

1 Sleep
Your body craves a regular routine especially when it comes to sleep. Create a routine that works for you with the aim of 7-9 hours sleep.

2 Eating Well
A routine of eating vegetables, fruits, lean meats and whole grains gives your body the nutrients for better function and balance your mental well-being as well.

3 Physical Exercise
A routine of daily exercise has both short term and long term benefits to your wellness and wellbeing, aim for 30 minutes a day of some activity you enjoy

4 Hygiene
- Hygiene includes both personal care and preventative medical care, so stay clean and fresh daily and don't put off those health checks

5 Relaxation

Whether it is getting a massage, staying home with a good book or playing your favourite sport, some "me time" does everyone good.

6 Stretch

Start your day and end your day with a head to toe stretch routine to keep you flexible and mobile.

7 Muscles

Develop strong muscle strength to help build healthier bones for good posture, back support, stability, balance, flexibility and a quicker healing process.

8 Health Visits

Conduct regular check ups on yourself and don't put off seeing a health professional for your health care.

Physical Wellness

To achieve optimal mental and physical health, you must balance exercise, sleep habits, nutrition and listening to your body when it is trying to tell you something.

Physical Wellness

Mental health and physical health go hand in hand. Looking good on the outside but feeling bad on the inside is not a healthy lifestyle – it's an unbalanced one. Physical wellness rebalances your overall health.

Notes

Notes

Notes

Notes

Spiritual Wellness

Spiritual Wellness
Find meaning in life events, demonstrate individual's purpose, and live a life that reflects your values and beliefs

Spiritual Wellness Tips

1 Values and Beliefs
Understand yourself, what are the values and core beliefs that drive you. How do they reflect in you behaviours.

2 Purpose
Reflect on your purpose, how does it align with your values, beliefs and behaviours. reflect on your identify and feel confident in your choices.

3 Self-Acceptance
Learn to accept yourself, for who you are not who you wish you were. You are unique be confident in who you are and the choices you make in life.

4 Gratitude
Being grateful for what you have in life that brings you joy, and peace will help bring calm, clarity and inner strength.

5 Be Mindful

Living in the moment teaches you to appreciate life and all its everyday pleasures and curiosities.

6 Successes and strengths

Look back over your life and identify your successes and the strengths that led you to them to reconnect to your personal journey to date and build your self esteem.

7 Other cultures

Experience other cultures whether that be through food, art, socialising, travel and deepen your human experience.

8 Trust

Learn to trust yourself knowing that you have the power and the tools to navigate this life effectively.

Spiritual Wellness

Spiritually well people use their own set of values, principles, morals and beliefs to guide their actions and decisions with confidence.

Spiritual Wellness

Our values and beliefs are at the
heart of everything we do.
For Spiritual wellness make time to
understand yours and manifest them
wisely for a healthy happy life.

Notes

Notes

Notes

Notes

Intellectual Wellness

Intellectual Wellness

Learn more, be open to new ideas, be creative, think critically, and seek out new challenges.

Intellectual Wellness Tips

1 Read for fun
Reading, especially something you enjoy, can improve your intellect by stretching your mind to think about things you normally don't think about!

2 Podcasts
Podcasts are also excellent ways to learn about new topics you may be interested in.

3 Learn a new skill
Whether it's cooking, gardening, crafting or building, learning a new skill is a fun and interactive way to improve your intellectual intelligence.

4 Time Management
Poor time management can lead to increased stress, affects all wellness areas. Being organised allows your mind to work more efficiently and effectively.

5 Create
Similar to the positive effects of reading, being creative is known to improve memory retention as well as emotional stability.

6 Try something new
Comfort zones are the prisons we inflict in ourselves through fear, try something new and starting strestching your confort zone.

7 Intelligence type
Identify your intelligence type using online assessments and learn ways to develop and learn that suit your type.

8 Learning style
Identify your learning style using online assessments and try learning things your interetsted in through your preferred learming style.

Intellectual Wellness

People that master mental stimulation by stretching their comfort zones and learning about things separate from their normal realm develop better wellness and wellbeing.

Intellectual Wellness

Brain health requires us to use our intelligence, cognitive and learning skills with our primitive need for evolution, to break free from self-inflicted limitations allowing us and our intellectual wellness to flourish.

Notes

Notes

Notes

Environmental Wellness

Environmental Wellness

Be aware of the interactions between the environment, community and yourself and behave in ways that care for each of these responsibly.

Environmental Wellness Tips

1 Declutter

Decluttering your space can help declutter our mind. Start one space at a time.

2 Get outside

Enjoying nature helps reduce stress, increase endorphins, and lets you appreciate the world around you.

3 Bring the outdoors inside

Plants can improve indoor air quality fresh air improves sleep. A dose of nature can enhance energy and performance.

4 Environmentally friendly

Ditching unnecessary chemicals, unhealthy foods, unfriendly Earth practices, and bad habits/routines will improve health and improve the environment and ecosystem.

5 Know your preferred environment
Know the environments that bring out the best in you and spend regular, quality time in them.

6 Carbon Footprint
Reduce your carbon footprint by cycling, walking or car sharing to get to work, school or college.

7 Upcycle
Use materials from old clothes to create comforting textiles for you home such as cushions, blankets and bags.

8 Reduce chemicals
Invest in eco cleaning products and hygiene products to reduce the chemicals in your home and attached to your body.

Environmental Wellness

Feeling as though you are in a safe and stimulating environment is a critical aspect of not only enhancing successes but also for your overall sense of wellbeing.

Environmental Wellness

The natural environment provides food, water, shelter and air needed for us to exist and flourish in the personal environments we create. For our environmental wellness we should respect both equally.

 **Notes**

Notes

Notes

Notes

Social Wellness

Social Wellness
Build relationships with others, deal with conflict appropriately, and connect to a positive social network.

Social Wellness Tips

1 Reflection

Reflect on yourself and your social needs. What aspects of your social life do you enjoy? What parts would you like to improve?

2 Support system

Take time to identify who your support systems are, the people who you share a 50/50 relationship with.

3 Keep in touch

Make time to keep in touch with the people in your support system. Keep those relationships strong.

4 Boundaries

Build healthy boundaries with people. Personal Boundaries are important because they set the basic guidelines of how you want to be treated.

5 Say Goodbye

Don't be scared of letting go of toxic people, how long someone has been in your life should not equate to how long you accept a negative relationship.

6 Community

Connect to your community whether that be joining a local group, shopping in your local shops or taking part in events.

7 Connect

Don't rely on social media to stay con-nected incorporate the classic ways too like chatting on a phone, meeting for a walk, popping in for a chat and a drink.

8 Communication

Develop your communication skills for better interactions and understanding of yourself an others.

Social Wellness

The relationships and support systems we build help us navigate our lives, in good times and in bad. It is important to establish positive and regular interactions with them.

Social Wellness

Developing healthy positive relationships requires open communication, empathy and personal accountability. It's the only control we have when it comes to people and when we accept that we start to develop social wellness.

 **Notes**

Notes

Notes

Notes

Occupational Wellness

Occupational Wellness
Seek to have a career that is interesting, enjoyable, meaningful and that contributes to the larger society.

Occupational Wellness Tips

---

1 Work life balance

Manage the waves of responsibility realistically and not choosing to only exist in one area of your life.

2 Don't settle

Stay motivated by continuing to set goals and work towards them whether it be with current employer, in your current role or in your current career.

3 Develop

Find ways to increase knowledge and skills to keep you motivated, interested and stimulated and remember to take responsibility for your own development.

4 Benefits

Identify and focus on the benefits to your current role, career. If you struggle to find any then you need to make a change.

5 Say Goodbye

Don't be scared of letting go if you are unhappy. Look for something new and/or talk to a career counsellor if you feel stuck or unhappy.

6 Fulfil potential

Showing potential is great in work it is what will get you noticed and possibly even promoted but remember to carry through and fulfil that potential.

7 Relationships

Develop and maintain good relationships with your colleagues as they will be forever part of your professional network.

8 Limitation

Don't limit your career or job opportunities by staying sat in your comfort zone; don't stay in a role you have outgrown, don't stay working for an employer that holds you back, don't say 'No' to things out of fear.

Occupational Wellness

Finding joy, purpose and satisfaction in your occupation leads to you enjoying what you do and is critical for your mental health and wellbeing.

Occupational Wellness

Work should not be 'who' we are,
it should be an 'extension' of who we
are. Our commitment to our work
becomes unhealthy when it also
becomes our identify.
Occupational wellness is when
we have that understanding and
manage our career by it.

Notes

Notes

Notes

Notes

Financial Wellness

Financial Wellness
Live within your means and learn to manage your finances for the short and long term.

Financial Wellness Tips

---

1 Relationship with money
Reflect on what money really means to you, and how it supports your values, beliefs, purpose and your overall wellbeing.

2 Financial literacy
Take time to learn the language of money, have the knowledge and skills to make effective decisions and develop money management tools.

3 Financial planning
Consider your current situation and then identify some clear goals and objectives for where you want your finances to be and why.

4 Money management
Track your monthly income and expenditure through a budget that is in a format of your choice and is user friendly for you.

5 Say Goodbye to the credit cycle
Understand credit/debt cycle traps including the difficulties and process for getting out of debt as well as the difficulties associated with gaining, maintaining and re-gaining good credit.

6 Commit to your credit reports
Check your credit report regularly even sign up for updates to have up to date information regarding your credit score and also potential fraud.

7 Plan for retirement
Plan for your life after you retire don't rely on just a pension scheme, you want to enjoy your retirement not be limited due to finances.

8 Protect what you have
Home insurance, health insurance and life insurance, these are all ways you can protect the life you live now and also those that you share your life with.

Financial Wellness

Understanding what money means to you will help you learn how to manage it helping you achieve financial satisfaction.

Financial Wellness

Money is a stress trigger, but why it triggers stress depends on what money means to you. For financial wellness understand the meaning of money to you and start to manage the stress linked to that meaning.

# Notes

Notes

 **Notes**

Notes

For more support, tips and information about 8Wise™ please follow us:

 Daltonwise.co.uk

 @8wisekim
@daltonwsiecoaching

 @8wise
@daltonwisecoachingandtherapy

 @8Wise_Kim
@daltonWiseCoach

 linkedin.com/company/dalton-wise-coaching-and-therapy

 pinterest.co.uk/daltonwiseltd/

ABOUT THE AUTHOR

Who better to be your 8Wise™ guide than its creator, Kim Rutherford, Co-founder of Dalton Wise Ltd, a mental health and wellness support service. Mental health has been a part of Kim's life since her childhood, it's what inspired her to become a psychotherapist and mental wellness coach, trainer and corporate consultant.

She is based in Liverpool, England where she uses 8Wise™ to help her clients take back control of their mental wellness and protect their longer term mental health.

www.ingramcontent.com/pod-product-compliance
Lightning Source LLC
Chambersburg PA
CBHW050507120526
44588CB00044B/1684